LEARN TO DRAW

Winnie the Pooh and Tigger

Illustrated by
David Pacheco
Pattie Tomsicek
Diana Wakeman

Walter Foster

Hi, Friends!

Wouldn't you love to be able to draw Winnie the Pooh and Tigger? This book will show you how. It's much easier than you'd think — and you'll have lots of fun while you learn! Let's take a quick look at the supplies you'll need. Then we can get started.

YOU'LL NEED A PENCIL TO DRAW. A NUMBER 2 IS BEST!

USE AN ERASER TO REMOVE ANY MISTAKES OR UNWANTED PENCIL LINES.

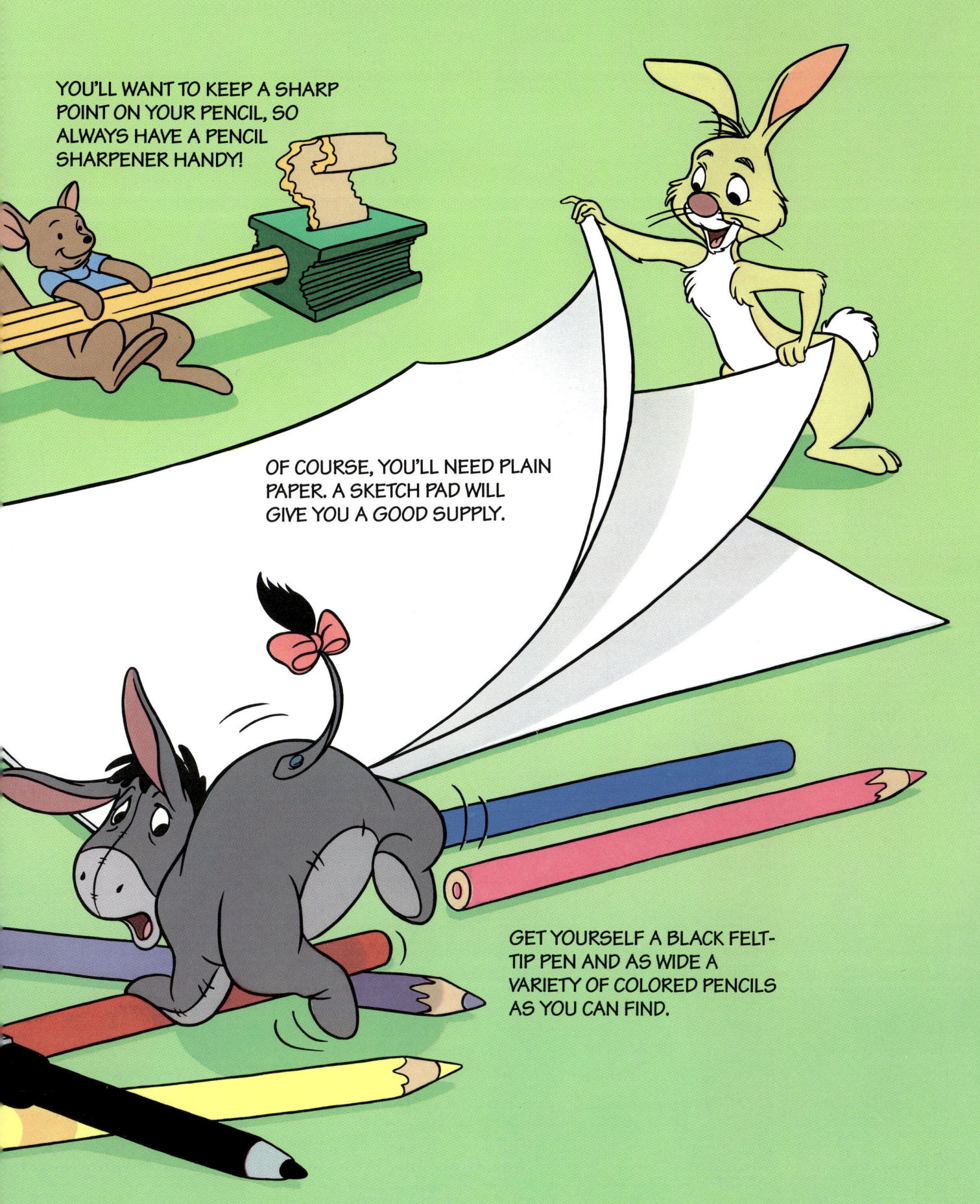

YOU'LL WANT TO KEEP A SHARP POINT ON YOUR PENCIL, SO ALWAYS HAVE A PENCIL SHARPENER HANDY!

OF COURSE, YOU'LL NEED PLAIN PAPER. A SKETCH PAD WILL GIVE YOU A GOOD SUPPLY.

GET YOURSELF A BLACK FELT-TIP PEN AND AS WIDE A VARIETY OF COLORED PENCILS AS YOU CAN FIND.

Getting the Right Shapes

You can draw Winnie the Pooh and Tigger using just a few simple shapes! Practice drawing these curved lines and shapes lightly, over and over, right on top of each other, until they look just right.

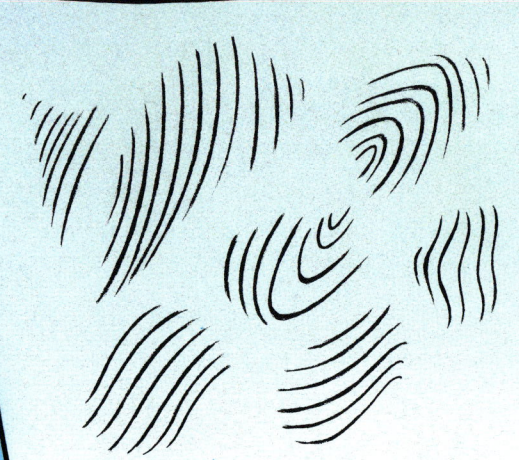

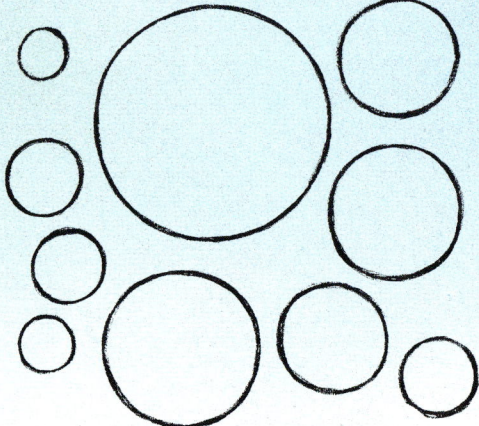

DRAW LINES WITH SHARP CURVES AND LINES WITH SMOOTH CURVES. DRAW LOTS OF CURVES TOGETHER.

MAKE CIRCLES BY LIGHTLY DRAWING AROUND AND AROUND. DRAW CIRCLES IN MANY DIFFERENT SIZES.

OVALS LOOK LIKE STRETCHED OR SQUASHED CIRCLES. DRAW OVALS IN DIFFERENT SIZES. DRAW FAT ONES AND THIN ONES.

DRAW CIRCLES AND CURVED LINES, JOINING THEM TO MAKE PEAR SHAPES. DRAW PEAR SHAPES OF DIFFERENT SIZES.

Let's Draw Pooh's Head

Now that you can draw the simple lines and shapes, let's try putting them together to make a drawing of Pooh's head. The blue lines show each new step of the drawing you will need to make.

 LIGHTLY DRAW A CIRCLE. DRAW TWO LINES THROUGH THE CENTER OF THE CIRCLE: ONE FROM TOP TO BOTTOM, AND THE OTHER FROM SIDE TO SIDE. THESE LINES WILL HELP YOU TO POSITION POOH'S FEATURES.

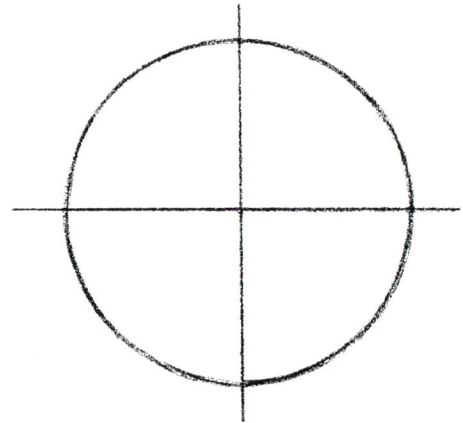

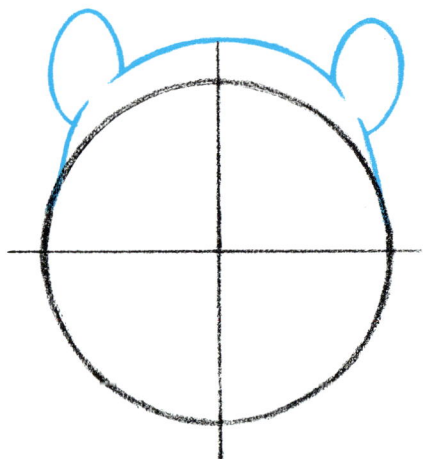 GIVE POOH'S FOREHEAD MORE HEIGHT BY DRAWING A CURVED LINE ABOVE THE TOP OF THE CIRCLE. ADD TWO OVALS FOR HIS EARS.

 DRAW A CURVED LINE BELOW AND BETWEEN THE EYES TO FORM THE TOP OF THE MUZZLE. ADD THE NOSE. NOTICE HOW THE VERTICAL CONSTRUCTION LINE DIVIDES THE NOSE AND MUZZLE.

 DRAW A CURVED LINE TO MAKE POOH'S SMILE. ADD SMALL CURVES TO FORM THE CORNERS OF THE MOUTH AND THE LOWER LIP.

Always remember to draw lightly. Use your eraser gently to remove any unwanted lines as you go along.

 POOH HAS A VERY FULL FACE. DRAW A CURVED LINE TO FORM THE CHEEKS AND CHIN. DID YOU NOTICE THAT THE CURVED LINE IS DRAWN WIDER AND LOWER THAN THE CONSTRUCTION CIRCLE?

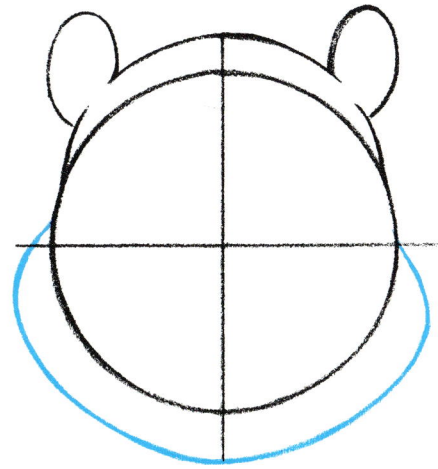

 SMALL OVALS FORM THE EYES. ADD SHORT, CURVED LINES ABOVE THE EYES TO FORM THE EYEBROWS, AND BELOW THE EYES TO INDICATE THE TOPS OF THE CHEEKS.

 CAREFULLY ERASE THE CONSTRUCTION LINES AND CLEAN UP THE DRAWING.

 OUTLINE POOH'S HEAD WITH YOUR BLACK FELT-TIP PEN. ONCE THE INK DRIES, COLOR HIM IN WITH YOUR COLORED PENCILS!

Let's Draw Tigger's Head

Tigger's head is different from Pooh's in many ways. Nevertheless, you'll find that you use the same basic lines and shapes to draw him.

1 START WITH A LIGHTLY DRAWN CIRCLE. ADD TWO LINES THAT PASS THROUGH THE CENTER, ONE FROM TOP TO BOTTOM, THE OTHER FROM SIDE TO SIDE. YOU'LL USE THESE LINES TO POSITION TIGGER'S FEATURES.

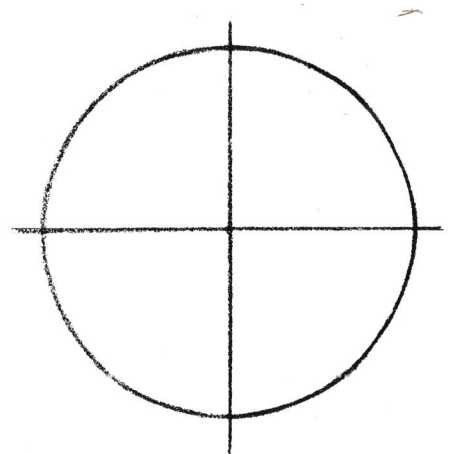

2 DRAW LONG, CURVING LINES THAT ARE WIDER THAN THE CIRCLE TO FORM THE TOP AND SIDES OF TIGGER'S HEAD. USE A VARIETY OF CURVED LINES TO DRAW HIS EARS.

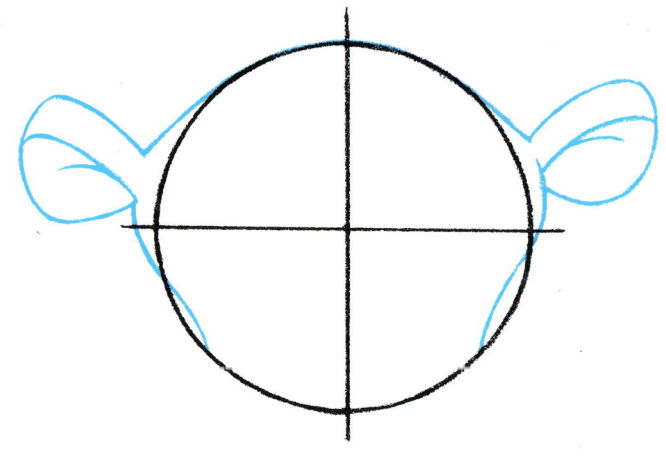

5 DRAW A LONG, CURVED LINE THAT GOES BELOW THE CONSTRUCTION CIRCLE TO FORM TIGGER'S CHIN. DRAW A SECOND CURVED LINE THAT DROPS A LITTLE BELOW THE CONSTRUCTION CIRCLE FOR HIS MOUTH.

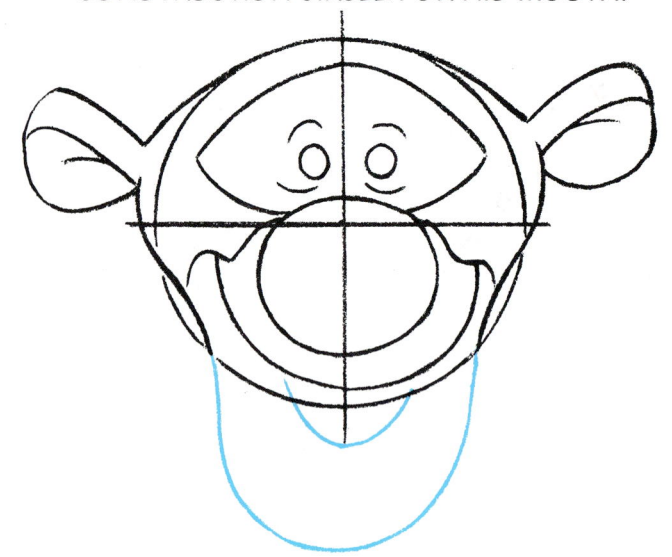

6 USE CURVED LINES TO ADD TIGGER'S STRIPES AND WHISKERS. BE SURE TO MAKE THE STRIPES LOOK AS IF THEY WRAP AROUND HIS HEAD. TRY TO GIVE SOME "BOUNCE" TO THE WHISKERS!

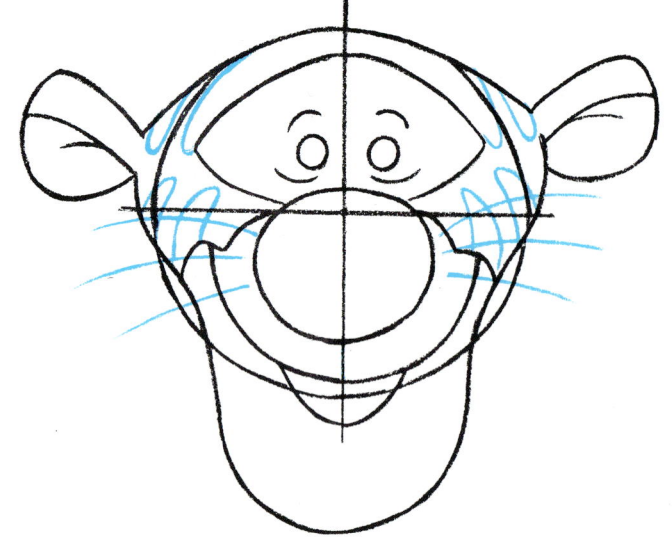

As before, the blue lines show the new steps you will need to make. Remember to keep your pencil sharp for the best results.

 TO DRAW TIGGER'S EYES, PLACE TWO SMALL CIRCLES ON EITHER SIDE OF THE VERTICAL CENTER LINE. ADD SHORT CURVES ABOVE AND BELOW THE EYES. DRAW A POINTED OVAL AREA AROUND THE EYES TO FORM TIGGER'S "MASK."

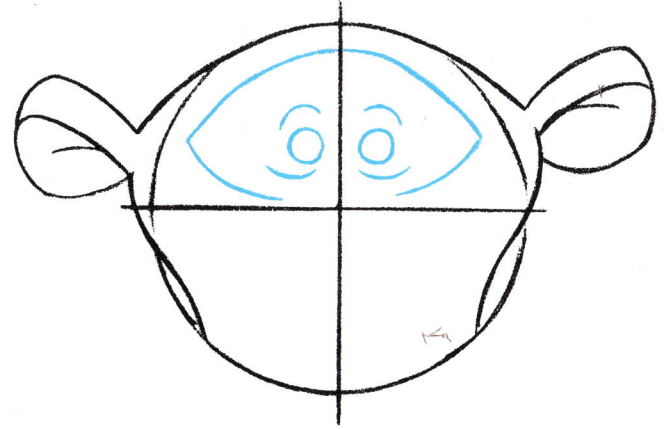

 DRAW TIGGER'S NOSE. ADD CURVED LINES FOR THE MUZZLE AND THE CHEEKS.

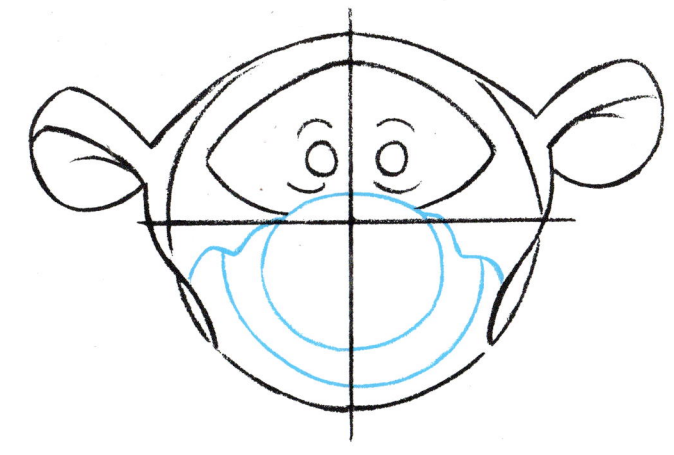

 GENTLY ERASE THE CONSTRUCTION LINES AND CLEAN UP THE DRAWING.

8 DRAW THE FINAL OUTLINE WITH YOUR FELT-TIP PEN, LET THE LINES DRY, AND THEN COLOR TIGGER WITH YOUR COLORED PENCILS. YOU'RE DONE!

The 3/4 View — Pooh

Of course you'll want to be able to draw Pooh's head from different angles. He looks nice and round when he's turned slightly to the side. Let's try drawing him that way!

1 LIGHTLY DRAW A CIRCLE. ADD TWO CURVED CENTER LINES THAT WRAP AROUND THE CIRCLE. TO MAKE POOH LOOK TO THE RIGHT, CURVE THE VERTICAL CENTER LINE OVER TO THAT SIDE.

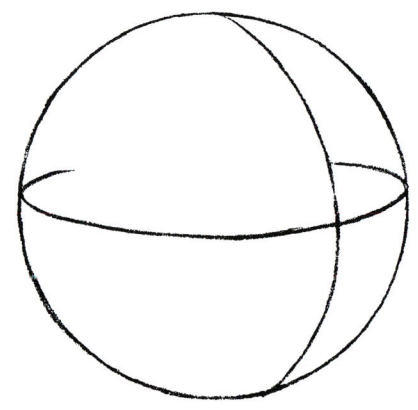

2 DRAW A CURVED LINE ABOVE THE CIRCLE TO FORM THE TOP OF POOH'S HEAD. NOTICE THAT THIS SHAPE IS SLIGHTLY SQUARED OFF. IT CONNECTS TO A LINE THAT SLOPES DOWN, INSIDE THE CIRCLE, TO FORM POOH'S FOREHEAD. ADD TWO OVALS FOR POOH'S EARS.

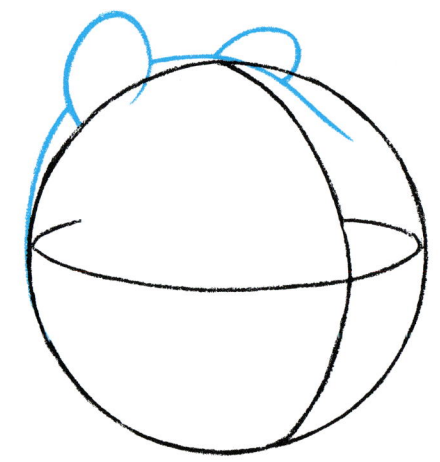

5 POOH'S MUZZLE IS A LONG, CURVING LINE THAT STARTS ABOVE HIS FAR EYE AND ENDS IN HIS CHEEK AREA. ADD HIS ROUNDED, TRIANGULAR NOSE, AND USE A SHORT CURVE FOR THE CORNER OF HIS MOUTH.

6 DRAW A VARIETY OF CURVED LINES TO FORM POOH'S MOUTH, LIP, AND TONGUE. USE THE VERTICAL CENTER LINE TO HELP YOU POSITION THEM.

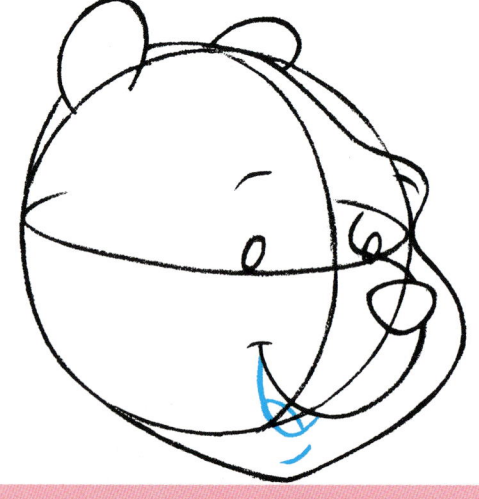

3 DRAW A SERIES OF CURVED LINES OUTSIDE THE CIRCLE TO FORM THE BROW, THE CHEEK, AND THE CHIN.

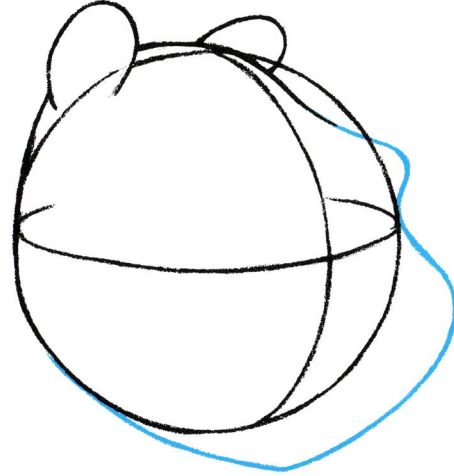

4 USING THE CENTER LINES FOR POSITION, DRAW TWO SMALL OVALS FOR POOH'S EYES. ADD SHORT, CURVED LINES FOR HIS EYEBROWS.

7 CAREFULLY ERASE THE CONSTRUCTION LINES AND CLEAN UP THE DRAWING.

8 OUTLINE CAREFULLY AND COLOR IN.

The 3/4 View — Tigger

The 3/4 view is a great angle for Tigger. There is a terrific sense of volume and it is the best angle to show Tigger's wide variety of expressions.

1 START BY LIGHTLY DRAWING A CIRCLE. WRAP TWO CURVED CENTER LINES AROUND IT. TO MAKE TIGGER LOOK TO THE LEFT, CURVE THE VERTICAL CENTER LINE OVER TO THAT SIDE.

2 DRAW HIS ROUNDED, TRIANGLE-SHAPED EARS ON THE SIDES OF HIS HEAD. ADD CURVED LINES TO SHOW THE INSIDES OF HIS EARS. NOTICE THAT THE EAR CLOSER TO US IS LARGER THAN THE ONE ON THE FAR SIDE OF THE HEAD.

5 ADD A LONG CURVED LINE TO FORM THE JAW AND ANOTHER FOR THE BOTTOM OF THE MOUTH.

6 USE A VARIETY OF CURVED LINES TO ADD TIGGER'S STRIPES AND WHISKERS. DRAW THE STRIPES SO THAT THEY HELP TO FORM THE SHAPE OF HIS HEAD.

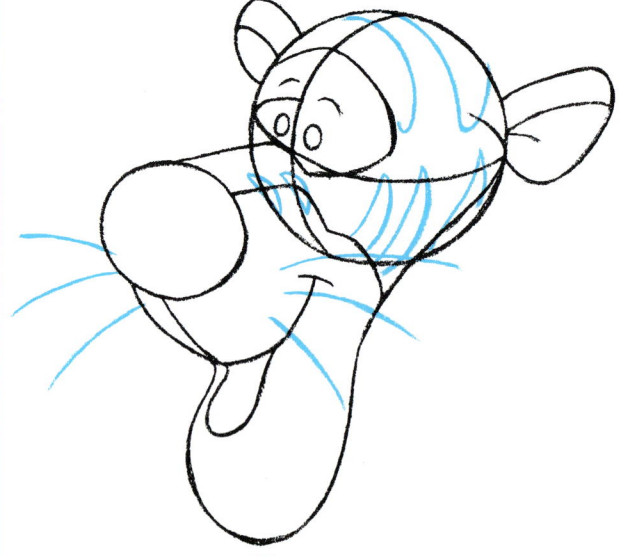

3 USE THE CENTER LINES TO POSITION TWO SMALL CIRCLES FOR THE EYES. ADD SHORT CURVES ABOVE AND BELOW TIGGER'S EYES. DRAW A POINTED OVAL SHAPE FOR THE MASK AROUND HIS EYES.

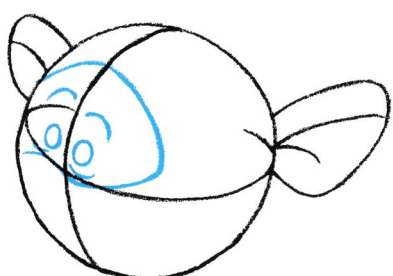

4 DRAW STRAIGHT AND CURVED LINES TO ADD TIGGER'S MUZZLE, MOUTH, AND CENTER LIP LINE. DRAW A FAT OVAL FOR HIS NOSE.

7 GENTLY ERASE THE CONSTRUCTION LINES AND CLEAN UP THE DRAWING.

8 CAREFULLY OUTLINE THE DRAWING AND LET THE INK DRY. NOW COLOR IN TIGGER WITH YOUR COLORED PENCILS!

Pooh's Expressions

Pooh's face is very soft and flexible. His eyebrows, nose, and mouth stretch and squash, changing shape to express his feelings. Notice how the tilt of his head also helps to reflect his attitude. Practice drawing the expressions Tigger has drawn below — then make some up yourself!

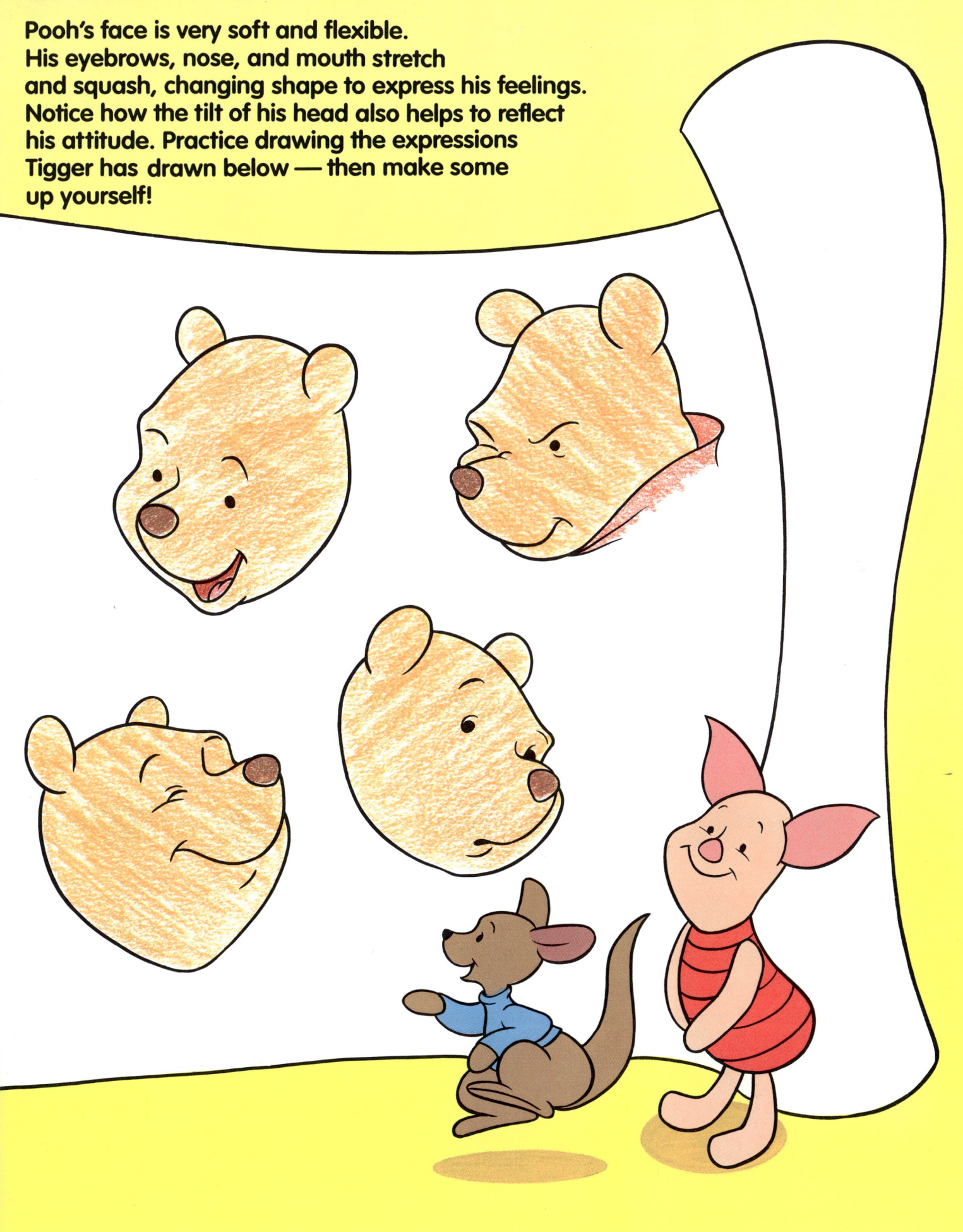

Pooh Standing

Pooh is three heads tall. This means if you draw three circles the size of Pooh's head, one on top of the other, you will get the height that Pooh should be.

1

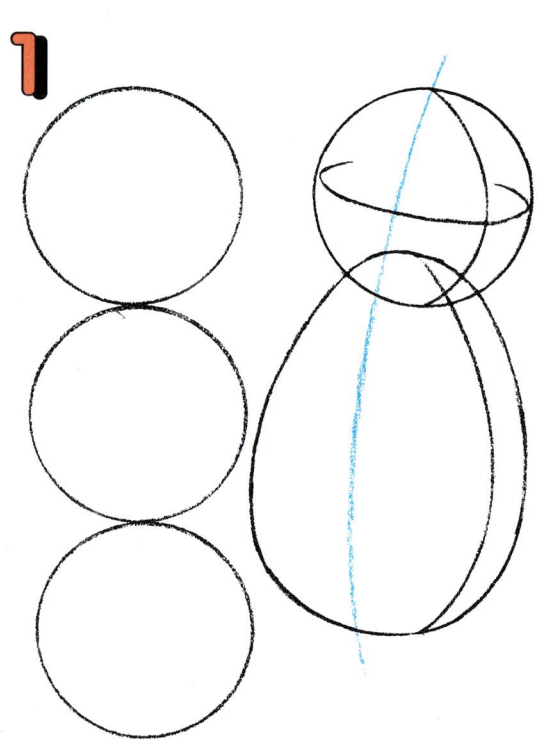

DRAW THE CURVED LINE OF ACTION. DRAW A CIRCLE FOR POOH'S HEAD. NOW DRAW AN EGG SHAPE FOR HIS BODY. ADD CURVED CENTER LINES.

2

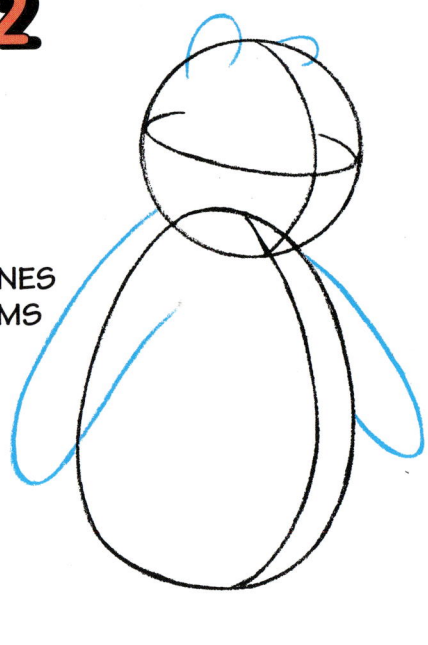

DRAW CURVED LINES TO FORM HIS ARMS AND EARS.

5

DRAW THE FEET NEXT. THE CURVES ON TOP SHOULD BE A LITTLE ROUNDER THAN ON THE BOTTOM.

6

DRAW POOH'S SHIRT SO THAT IT COVERS THE TOP THIRD OF HIS BODY. GIVE THE BOTTOM OF THE SHIRT A NICE CURVE AS IT WRAPS AROUND HIS BODY.

When you draw Pooh standing, start by drawing a line of action. The line of action is a guideline to help you give your character direction and movement.

3

DRAW POOH'S LEGS. THEY ARE LIKE STRETCHED OUT OVALS THAT ARE TOP HEAVY AND ARE ATTACHED TOWARD THE BACK OF HIS BODY.

4

DRAW THE FACIAL FEATURES AS YOU LEARNED BEFORE.

7

CAREFULLY ERASE THE CONSTRUCTION LINES AND CLEAN UP THE DRAWING.

8

OUTLINE POOH WITH YOUR BLACK FELT-TIP PEN, AND COLOR HIM IN!

Tigger Standing

Tigger is 5 1/2 heads tall. This means that if you stack 5 1/2 balls the size of Tigger's head, one on top of the other, that is how tall Tigger should be.

1

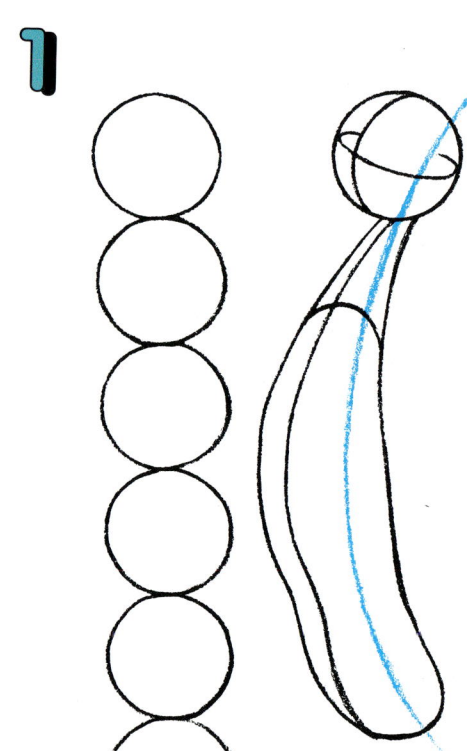

LIGHTLY DRAW THE LINE OF ACTION. DRAW A CIRCLE FOR THE HEAD. TIGGER'S BODY IS LIKE A LONG OVAL WITH SLIGHT CURVES FOR HIS WAIST AND BACK. DRAW A NARROW CONE SHAPE FOR THE NECK. ADD CENTER LINES.

2

DRAW THE EARS AS YOU ALREADY LEARNED. USE CURVED LINES TO FORM THE ARMS.

5

USE CURVED LINES TO DRAW TIGGER'S HANDS AND FEET.

6

DRAW TIGGER'S CURVED TAIL. KEEP THE TAIL ANGULAR, AS IF A SPRING IS COILED INSIDE. DRAW CURVED LINES FOR THE STRIPES AROUND THE TAIL AND BODY. USE THEM TO HELP DEFINE THE BODY CONTOURS.

As with Pooh, you should begin by drawing a line of action. This will help you to give your character direction and movement.

3
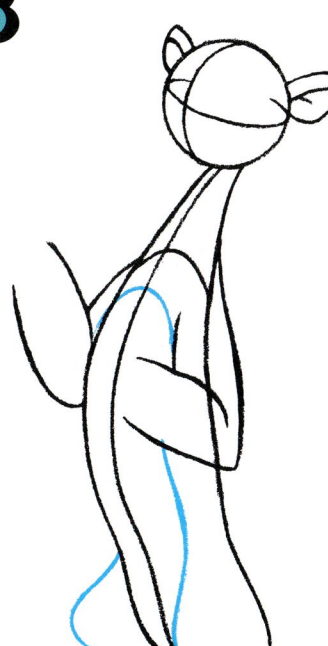

DRAW CURVED LINES TO FORM THE SHORT, BENT LEGS. TIGGER'S CHEST AREA IS A SEPARATE COLOR. USE A CURVED LINE TO SHOW HIS CHEST.

4

NOW DRAW IN THE FACIAL FEATURES, THE STRIPES, AND THE WHISKERS AS YOU LEARNED BEFORE.

7

GENTLY ERASE THE CONSTRUCTION LINES AND CLEAN UP THE DRAWING.

8

USE YOUR FELT-TIP PEN TO OUTLINE THE DRAWING. NOW YOU'RE READY TO COLOR IN TIGGER!

Tigger's Expressions

Tigger is a lively, fun character. He makes various facial expressions by squashing and stretching his features. You can make him look angry, pleased, questioning, or smug.

TRY DRAWING THESE EXPRESSIONS, OR TRY A FEW NEW ONES ON YOUR OWN. REMEMBER TIGGER IS ENTHUSIASTIC, OVER-CONFIDENT, BOUNCY, AND JUST PLAIN HAPPY-GO-LUCKY.

The Tigger Shuffle
Pooh Walking

You've drawn Pooh and Tigger standing still, now let's set the two of them in motion! You'll use the same simple shapes and follow similar steps.

1 DRAW THE LINE OF ACTION. DRAW A CIRCLE WITH CENTER LINES CURVED TOWARD THE TOP OF THE CIRCLE. THIS WILL TILT TIGGER'S HEAD UPWARD. DRAW HIS BODY LEANING LEFT. ADD HIS NECK AND THE CENTER LINES.

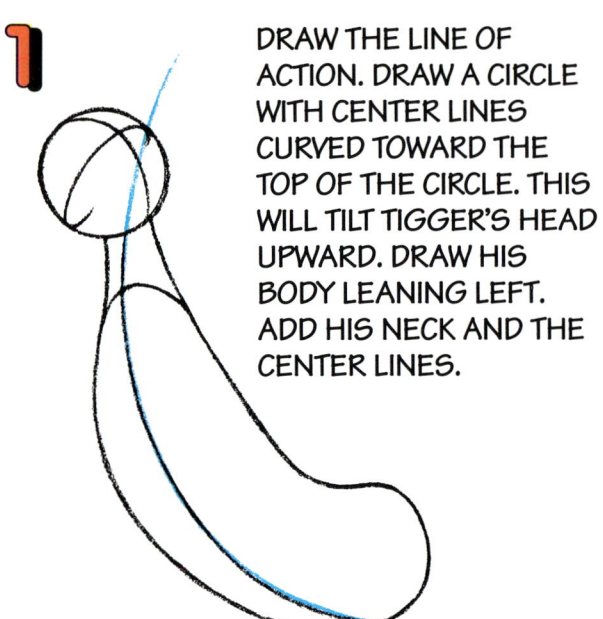

2 ATTACH TIGGER'S TUBE-LIKE ARMS AND SHORT, ROUNDED LEGS. ADD THE HANDS, FEET, AND EARS.

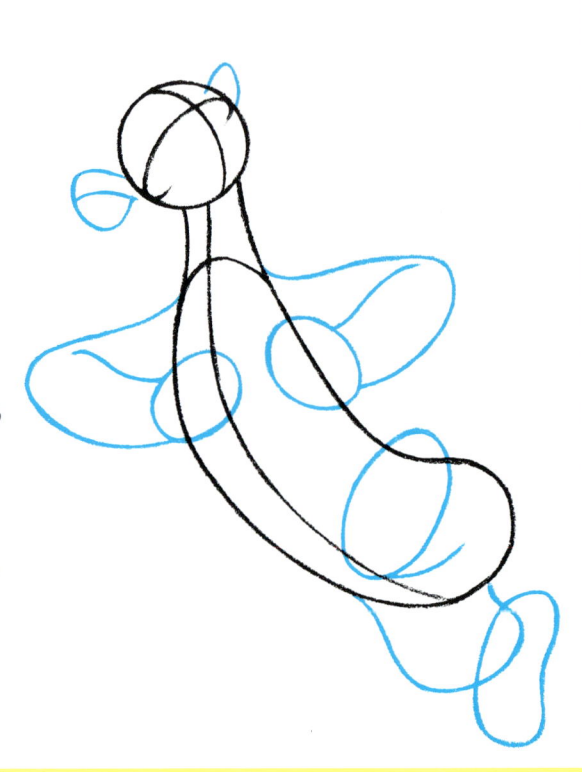

1 LIGHTLY DRAW THE LINE OF ACTION. DRAW A CIRCLE FOR THE HEAD AND A LARGE PEAR SHAPE FOR THE BODY. ADD CURVED CENTER LINES.

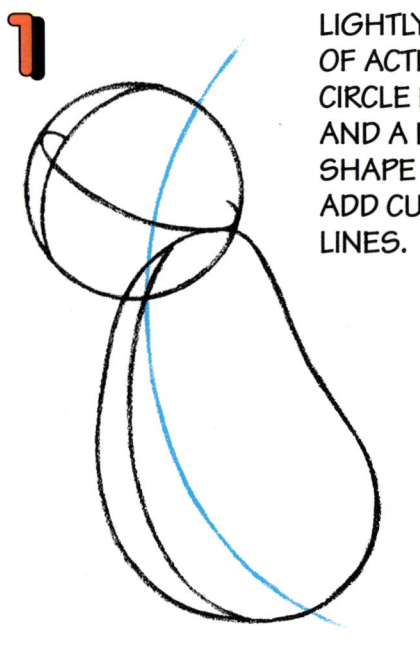

2 ADD THE ROUNDED SHAPES OF THE ARMS, LEGS, AND FEET.

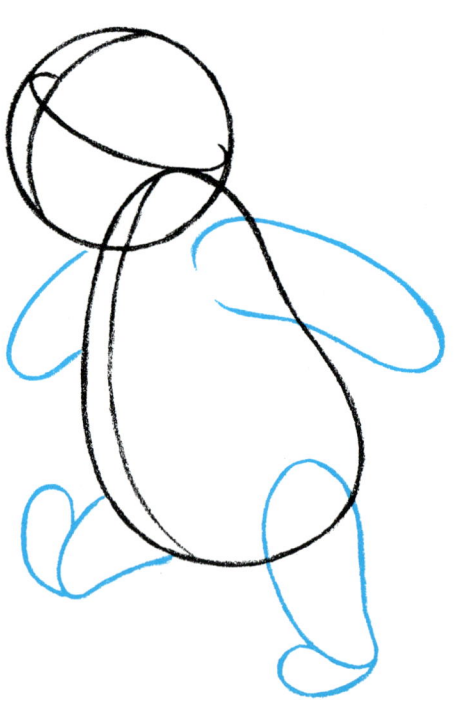

3.  DRAW IN HIS TAIL AND ALL THE DETAILS AS YOU PREVIOUSLY LEARNED.

4. ERASE THE CONSTRUCTION LINES, OUTLINE TIGGER, AND COLOR HIM IN!

3.  DRAW IN THE FACIAL FEATURES AND THE SHIRT AS YOU LEARNED BEFORE.

4. CAREFULLY ERASE THE UNWANTED LINES. OUTLINE POOH AND FINISH HIM WITH COLOR!

Action Poses

Both Pooh and Tigger are very lively, playful characters. Practice drawing the action poses below and then make up some of your own.

It may help to imagine yourself in these activities. You can even look at yourself in a mirror for ideas!

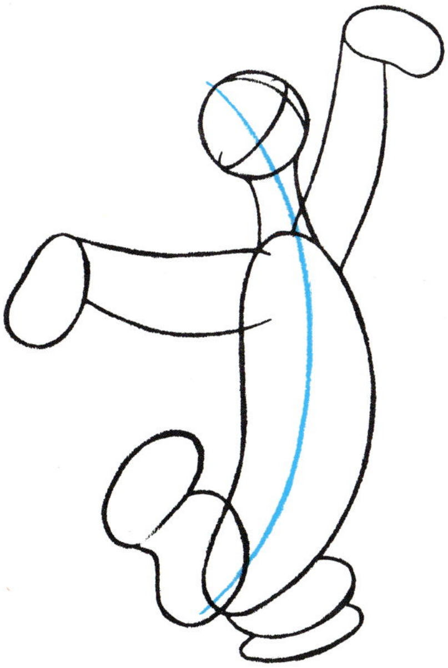

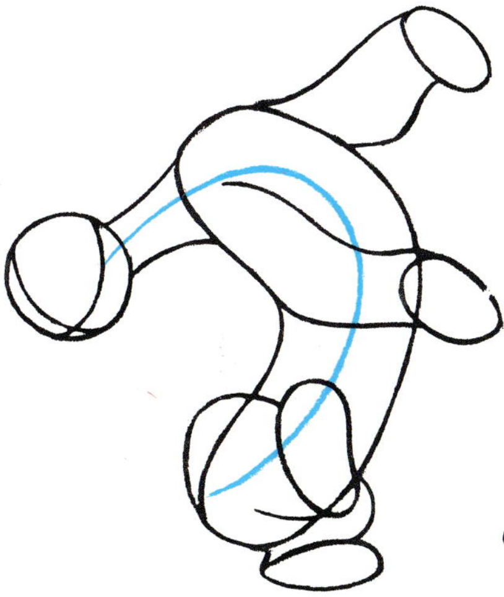

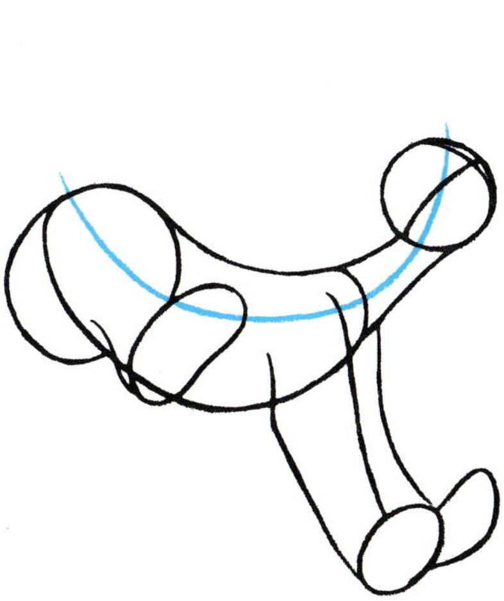

Coloring Techniques

Here are some tips to help you get the best results with your colored pencils.

TIGGER USES THE TIP OF HIS COLORED PENCIL TO COLOR IN THE SMALLER AREAS OF POOH. RABBIT USES THE SIDE OF HIS COLORED PENCIL TO COVER THE LARGE AREAS QUICKLY AND EVENLY.

WHY NOT PROVIDE A SETTING FOR YOUR CHARACTERS? POOH'S SUGGESTED A WHOLE WORLD FOR TIGGER TO PLAY IN BY SIMPLY DRAWING IN A FEW TUFTS OF GRASS AND SOME FLOWERS AROUND HIS FEET.

Other Methods Of Coloring

There are lots of other techniques and materials you can use to add color to your drawings.

PIGLET'S USING A BRUSH AND A TRAY OF WATERCOLORS TO FINISH OFF A PORTRAIT OF POOH. HE CAN GET SOME SOFT, SUBTLE EFFECTS USING THESE MATERIALS.

EEYORE AND ROO ARE GETTING SPLENDID RESULTS AS THEY PAINT IN BRIGHT COLORS WITH THEIR POSTER PAINTS!

TIGGER'S DONE A GREAT JOB WITH HIS COLORED FELT-TIP MARKERS! HE LOOKS PRETTY PLEASED WITH THE BRILLIANT COLORS.